MW00930351

# 365 DAYS PROJECT

This notebook belongs to:

- - - - - - - - - - - - - - - - -

# Example

## IDEAS :

Here's some space to write down the plans and ideas for your daily photo's.

Brainstorm ideas or make a list of things you need for the photo shoot. Just write down what is useful to you.

On the right you can make a small sketch of the image you have in your head.

My Favorite Cacti

## SUBJECT :

Take a Photo of Your Favorite Plant

Place your subject in the empty space on the left.

It can be one of the subjects from the subject list at the back of the book, which you can cut and paste into place. Or you can write or draw something yourself. It can also be something that inspires you, such as a newspaper article or magazine photo. Be creative !

*1*

IDEAS :

SUBJECT :

*2*

IDEAS :

_____
_____
_____
_____
_____
_____
_____
_____
_____

_____
_____
_____
_____

SUBJECT :

_____
_____
_____
_____
_____
_____
_____
_____
_____
_____
_____
_____
_____
_____

# 3

IDEAS :

SUBJECT :

4

IDEAS :

SUBJECT :

5

IDEAS :
_____
_____
_____
_____
_____
_____
_____
_____
_____
_____

_____
_____
_____

SUBJECT :
_____
_____
_____
_____
_____
_____
_____
_____
_____
_____
_____

# 6

_____
_____
_____
_____
_____
_____
_____
_____
_____
_____
_____
_____

SUBJECT :

_____
_____
_____
_____
_____
_____
_____
_____
_____
_____
_____

7

IDEAS :

_____
_____
_____
_____
_____
_____
_____
_____
_____
_____
_____
_____
_____

SUBJECT :

_____
_____
_____
_____
_____
_____
_____
_____
_____
_____
_____
_____
_____
_____

IDEAS :

_____
_____
_____
_____
_____
_____
_____
_____
_____
_____
_____
_____
_____

SUBJECT :

# 10

IDEAS :

SUBJECT :

*11*

IDEAS :

_____
_____
_____
_____
_____
_____
_____
_____
_____

_____
_____
_____

SUBJECT :

_____
_____
_____
_____
_____
_____
_____
_____
_____
_____
_____
_____

*12*

IDEAS :

SUBJECT :

## 13

_____
_____
_____
_____
_____
_____
_____
_____
_____

_____
_____
_____

SUBJECT :

_____
_____
_____
_____
_____
_____
_____
_____
_____
_____
_____
_____

# 14

IDEAS :

_____
_____
_____
_____
_____
_____
_____
_____
_____
_____
_____

SUBJECT :

_____
_____
_____
_____
_____
_____
_____
_____
_____
_____

*15*

16

IDEAS :

_____

SUBJECT :

# 17

IDEAS :

_____
_____
_____
_____
_____
_____
_____
_____

_____
_____
_____

SUBJECT :

_____
_____
_____
_____
_____
_____
_____
_____
_____
_____
_____
_____
_____

*18*

19

*20*

IDEAS :

_____

_____

_____

_____

_____

_____

_____

_____

_____

_____

_____

_____

SUBJECT :

_____

_____

_____

_____

_____

_____

_____

_____

_____

_____

_____

_____

**21**

IDEAS :

_____
_____
_____
_____
_____
_____
_____
_____
_____

_____
_____
_____

SUBJECT :

_____
_____
_____
_____
_____
_____
_____
_____
_____
_____
_____

# 22

IDEAS :

_____
_____
_____
_____
_____
_____
_____
_____
_____
_____
_____
_____

SUBJECT :

_____
_____
_____
_____
_____
_____
_____
_____
_____
_____
_____

# 23

IDEAS :

_____
_____
_____
_____
_____
_____
_____
_____
_____

_____
_____
_____

SUBJECT :

_____
_____
_____
_____
_____
_____
_____
_____
_____
_____
_____
_____
_____

## 24

IDEAS :

_____
_____
_____
_____
_____
_____
_____
_____
_____
_____
_____
_____

SUBJECT :

_____
_____
_____
_____
_____
_____
_____
_____
_____
_____
_____
_____

**25**

IDEAS :

_____
_____
_____
_____
_____
_____
_____
_____
_____
_____
_____
_____

SUBJECT :

_____
_____
_____
_____
_____
_____
_____
_____
_____
_____
_____
_____

# 26

IDEAS :

_____

SUBJECT :

# 27

IDEAS :

_____
_____
_____
_____
_____
_____
_____
_____
_____
_____
_____

SUBJECT :

_____
_____
_____
_____
_____
_____
_____
_____
_____
_____
_____

# 28

IDEAS :

_____

_____

_____

_____

_____

_____

_____

_____

_____

_____

_____

SUBJECT :

_____

_____

_____

_____

_____

_____

_____

_____

_____

_____

# 29

# 30

IDEAS :

_____
_____
_____
_____
_____
_____
_____
_____
_____

_____
_____

SUBJECT :

_____
_____
_____
_____
_____
_____
_____
_____
_____
_____

# 31

32

IDEAS :

_____

_____

_____

_____

_____

_____

_____

_____

_____

_____

_____

_____

SUBJECT :

_____

_____

_____

_____

_____

_____

_____

_____

_____

_____

_____

_____

# 33

IDEAS :

SUBJECT :

# 34

35

IDEAS :

SUBJECT :

# 36

SUBJECT :

37

# 38

IDEAS :

SUBJECT :

# 39

IDEAS :

_____
_____
_____
_____
_____
_____
_____
_____
_____
_____
_____

SUBJECT :

_____
_____
_____
_____
_____
_____
_____
_____
_____
_____
_____

# 40

IDEAS :

_____
_____
_____
_____
_____
_____
_____
_____
_____

_____
_____
_____
_____

SUBJECT :

_____
_____
_____
_____
_____
_____
_____
_____
_____
_____
_____
_____

# 41

42

IDEAS :

_____
_____
_____
_____
_____
_____
_____
_____
_____

_____
_____
_____

SUBJECT :

_____
_____
_____
_____
_____
_____
_____
_____
_____
_____
_____

# 43

_____
_____
_____
_____
_____
_____
_____
_____
_____

_____
_____
_____

SUBJECT :

_____
_____
_____
_____
_____
_____
_____
_____
_____
_____
_____
_____

# 44

SUBJECT :

45

## 46

IDEAS :

_____

_____

_____

_____

_____

_____

_____

_____

_____

_____

_____

SUBJECT :

_____

_____

_____

_____

_____

_____

_____

_____

_____

_____

_____

47

48

IDEAS :

_____
_____
_____
_____
_____
_____
_____
_____
_____
_____
_____
_____

SUBJECT :

_____
_____
_____
_____
_____
_____
_____
_____
_____
_____
_____

49

# 50

IDEAS :

_____

_____

_____

_____

_____

_____

_____

_____

_____

_____

_____

_____

SUBJECT :

_____

_____

_____

_____

_____

_____

_____

_____

_____

_____

_____

_____

_____

# 51

_____
_____
_____
_____
_____
_____
_____
_____
_____

_____
_____
_____

SUBJECT :

_____
_____
_____
_____
_____
_____
_____
_____
_____
_____
_____
_____
_____

*52*

IDEAS :

_____
_____
_____
_____
_____
_____
_____
_____
_____
_____
_____
_____

SUBJECT :

_____
_____
_____
_____
_____
_____
_____
_____
_____
_____
_____
_____

# 53

IDEAS :

_____
_____
_____
_____
_____
_____
_____
_____
_____

_____
_____
_____

SUBJECT :

_____
_____
_____
_____
_____
_____
_____
_____
_____
_____
_____
_____
_____
_____

# 54

SUBJECT :

## 55

_____
_____
_____
_____
_____
_____
_____
_____
_____

_____
_____
_____

SUBJECT :

_____
_____
_____
_____
_____
_____
_____
_____
_____
_____
_____
_____

## 56

IDEAS :

_____
_____
_____
_____
_____
_____
_____
_____
_____
_____
_____
_____

SUBJECT :

_____
_____
_____
_____
_____
_____
_____
_____
_____
_____
_____
_____
_____

57

SUBJECT :

58

IDEAS :

SUBJECT :

59

IDEAS :

_____
_____
_____
_____
_____
_____
_____
_____
_____

_____
_____
_____

SUBJECT :

_____
_____
_____
_____
_____
_____
_____
_____
_____
_____
_____
_____

61

IDEAS :

SUBJECT :

62

IDEAS :

_____
_____
_____
_____
_____
_____
_____
_____
_____

_____
_____
_____

SUBJECT :

_____
_____
_____
_____
_____
_____
_____
_____
_____
_____
_____
_____

63

IDEAS :

SUBJECT :

65

_____
_____
_____
_____
_____
_____
_____
_____
_____
_____
_____
_____
_____

SUBJECT :

_____
_____
_____
_____
_____
_____
_____
_____
_____
_____
_____
_____

IDEAS :

_____
_____
_____
_____
_____
_____
_____
_____
_____
_____
_____
_____
_____

SUBJECT :

_____
_____
_____
_____
_____
_____
_____
_____
_____
_____
_____
_____
_____

67

SUBJECT :

68

IDEAS :

SUBJECT :

69

76

IDEAS :

SUBJECT :

# 71

_____
_____
_____
_____
_____
_____
_____
_____
_____

_____
_____
_____

SUBJECT :

_____
_____
_____
_____
_____
_____
_____
_____
_____
_____
_____
_____
_____

72

73

_____
_____
_____
_____
_____
_____
_____
_____
_____

_____
_____
_____

SUBJECT :

_____
_____
_____
_____
_____
_____
_____
_____
_____
_____
_____
_____

# 74

IDEAS :

_____
_____
_____
_____
_____
_____
_____
_____
_____

_____
_____
_____

SUBJECT :

_____
_____
_____
_____
_____
_____
_____
_____
_____
_____
_____
_____
_____

# 75

IDEAS :

_____

_____

_____

_____

_____

_____

_____

_____

_____

_____

_____

SUBJECT :

_____

_____

_____

_____

_____

_____

_____

_____

_____

_____

_____

_____

_____

76

IDEAS :

SUBJECT :

IDEAS :

_____
_____
_____
_____
_____
_____
_____
_____
_____

_____
_____
_____

SUBJECT :

_____
_____
_____
_____
_____
_____
_____
_____
_____
_____
_____
_____
_____
_____

78

IDEAS :

_____
_____
_____
_____
_____
_____
_____
_____
_____
_____
_____
_____
_____

SUBJECT :

_____
_____
_____
_____
_____
_____
_____
_____
_____
_____
_____

IDEAS :

SUBJECT :

80

IDEAS :

_____
_____
_____
_____
_____
_____
_____
_____
_____

_____
_____
_____
_____

SUBJECT :

_____
_____
_____
_____
_____
_____
_____
_____
_____
_____
_____

81

SUBJECT :

**82**

IDEAS :

_____
_____
_____
_____
_____
_____
_____
_____

_____
_____
_____

SUBJECT :

_____
_____
_____
_____
_____
_____
_____
_____
_____
_____

83

IDEAS :

_____

_____

_____

_____

_____

_____

_____

_____

_____

_____

_____

SUBJECT :

_____

_____

_____

_____

_____

_____

_____

_____

_____

_____

_____

_____

_____

_____

*84*

IDEAS :

SUBJECT :

IDEAS :

_____
_____
_____
_____
_____
_____
_____
_____
_____
_____
_____
_____
_____

SUBJECT :

_____
_____
_____
_____
_____
_____
_____
_____
_____
_____
_____
_____
_____

86

IDEAS :

_____
_____
_____
_____
_____
_____
_____
_____
_____

_____
_____
_____

SUBJECT :

_____
_____
_____
_____
_____
_____
_____
_____
_____
_____
_____

87

IDEAS :

SUBJECT :

## 88

IDEAS :

_____
_____
_____
_____
_____
_____
_____
_____
_____
_____
_____
_____

SUBJECT :

_____
_____
_____
_____
_____
_____
_____
_____
_____
_____

89

IDEAS :

_____
_____
_____
_____
_____
_____
_____
_____
_____
_____
_____
_____
_____

SUBJECT :

_____
_____
_____
_____
_____
_____
_____
_____
_____
_____
_____
_____
_____

IDEAS :

_____
_____
_____
_____
_____
_____
_____
_____
_____

_____
_____
_____
_____

SUBJECT :

_____
_____
_____
_____
_____
_____
_____
_____
_____
_____
_____
_____

91

SUBJECT :

IDEAS :

SUBJECT :

93

94

IDEAS :

SUBJECT :

95

IDEAS :

_____
_____
_____
_____
_____
_____
_____
_____
_____

_____
_____
_____

SUBJECT :

_____
_____
_____
_____
_____
_____
_____
_____
_____
_____
_____
_____
_____
_____

IDEAS :

SUBJECT :

IDEAS :

SUBJECT :

98

# 99

IDEAS :

_____
_____
_____
_____
_____
_____
_____
_____
_____
_____
_____
_____

SUBJECT :

_____
_____
_____
_____
_____
_____
_____
_____
_____
_____
_____
_____

# 100

IDEAS :

_____
_____
_____
_____
_____
_____
_____
_____
_____
_____
_____
_____

SUBJECT :

_____
_____
_____
_____
_____
_____
_____
_____
_____
_____
_____
_____
_____

# 101

IDEAS :

_____
_____
_____
_____
_____
_____
_____
_____
_____

_____
_____
_____

SUBJECT :

_____
_____
_____
_____
_____
_____
_____
_____
_____
_____
_____
_____
_____
_____

IDEAS :

_____
_____
_____
_____
_____
_____
_____
_____
_____
_____
_____

SUBJECT :

_____
_____
_____
_____
_____
_____
_____
_____
_____
_____
_____

# 103

IDEAS :

_____
_____
_____
_____
_____
_____
_____
_____
_____
_____
_____
_____

SUBJECT :

_____
_____
_____
_____
_____
_____
_____
_____
_____
_____
_____

# 104

IDEAS :

SUBJECT :

IDEAS :

SUBJECT :

107

IDEAS :

_____
_____
_____
_____
_____
_____
_____
_____
_____
_____
_____
_____
_____

SUBJECT :

_____
_____
_____
_____
_____
_____
_____
_____
_____
_____
_____
_____
_____

IDEAS :

_____
_____
_____
_____
_____
_____
_____
_____
_____
_____
_____
_____

SUBJECT :

_____
_____
_____
_____
_____
_____
_____
_____
_____
_____

## 109

IDEAS :

_____
_____
_____
_____
_____
_____
_____
_____
_____

_____
_____

SUBJECT :

_____
_____
_____
_____
_____
_____
_____
_____
_____
_____
_____

IDEAS :

SUBJECT :

*111*

SUBJECT :

IDEAS :

SUBJECT :

*113*

IDEAS :

_____

_____

_____

_____

_____

_____

_____

_____

_____

_____

_____

_____

_____

SUBJECT :

_____

_____

_____

_____

_____

_____

_____

_____

_____

_____

_____

_____

114

IDEAS :

_____
_____
_____
_____
_____
_____
_____
_____
_____

_____
_____
_____

SUBJECT :

_____
_____
_____
_____
_____
_____
_____
_____
_____
_____
_____
_____

# 116

IDEAS :

_____
_____
_____
_____
_____
_____
_____
_____
_____
_____
_____
_____

SUBJECT :

_____
_____
_____
_____
_____
_____
_____
_____
_____
_____
_____
_____
_____

117

118

IDEAS :

SUBJECT :

119

126

121

SUBJECT :

122

123

_____
_____
_____
_____
_____
_____
_____
_____
_____
_____
_____
_____

SUBJECT :

_____
_____
_____
_____
_____
_____
_____
_____
_____
_____
_____
_____
_____

124

125

126

# 127

IDEAS :

_____

_____

_____

_____

_____

_____

_____

_____

_____

_____

_____

_____

_____

SUBJECT :

_____

_____

_____

_____

_____

_____

_____

_____

_____

_____

_____

_____

_____

IDEAS :

SUBJECT :

129

IDEAS :

SUBJECT :

131

SUBJECT :

132

IDEAS :

SUBJECT :

# 133

IDEAS :

_____
_____
_____
_____
_____
_____
_____
_____
_____
_____
_____
_____
_____

SUBJECT :

_____
_____
_____
_____
_____
_____
_____
_____
_____
_____
_____
_____

IDEAS :

_____
_____
_____
_____
_____
_____
_____
_____
_____
_____
_____
_____

SUBJECT :

_____
_____
_____
_____
_____
_____
_____
_____
_____
_____
_____
_____
_____

135

# 136

IDEAS :

SUBJECT :

# 137

IDEAS :

_____
_____
_____
_____
_____
_____
_____
_____
_____
_____
_____
_____
_____

SUBJECT :

_____
_____
_____
_____
_____
_____
_____
_____
_____
_____
_____
_____
_____

# 138

IDEAS :

_____
_____
_____
_____
_____
_____
_____
_____
_____
_____
_____
_____
_____

SUBJECT :

_____
_____
_____
_____
_____
_____
_____
_____
_____
_____
_____
_____

139

IDEAS :

SUBJECT :

IDEAS :

SUBJECT :

# 141

SUBJECT :

# 142

# 143

IDEAS :

_____
_____
_____
_____
_____
_____
_____
_____
_____

_____
_____
_____

SUBJECT :

_____
_____
_____
_____
_____
_____
_____
_____
_____
_____
_____
_____

144

145

146

# 147

_____
_____
_____
_____
_____
_____
_____
_____
_____
_____
_____
_____

SUBJECT :

_____
_____
_____
_____
_____
_____
_____
_____
_____
_____
_____
_____

# 148

IDEAS :

SUBJECT :

# 149

_____
_____
_____
_____
_____
_____
_____
_____

_____
_____
_____

SUBJECT :

_____
_____
_____
_____
_____
_____
_____
_____
_____
_____
_____

150

# 151

_____
_____
_____
_____
_____
_____
_____
_____
_____
_____

_____
_____
_____

_____
_____
_____
_____
_____
_____
_____
_____
_____
_____
_____

152

SUBJECT :

# 153

IDEAS :

SUBJECT :

154

# 155

156

IDEAS :

SUBJECT :

158

IDEAS :

SUBJECT :

# 159

_____
_____
_____
_____
_____
_____
_____
_____
_____

_____
_____
_____
_____

SUBJECT :

_____
_____
_____
_____
_____
_____
_____
_____
_____
_____
_____
_____
_____

IDEAS :

SUBJECT :

IDEAS :

_____
_____
_____
_____
_____
_____
_____
_____
_____

_____
_____
_____

SUBJECT :

                              _____
                              _____
                              _____
                              _____
                              _____
                              _____
                              _____
                              _____
                              _____
                              _____
                              _____
                              _____

# 162

IDEAS :

SUBJECT :

# 163

_____

_____

_____

_____

_____

_____

_____

_____

_____

_____

_____

_____

SUBJECT :

_____

_____

_____

_____

_____

_____

_____

_____

_____

_____

_____

164

# 165

IDEAS :

_____
_____
_____
_____
_____
_____
_____
_____
_____
_____
_____

SUBJECT :

_____
_____
_____
_____
_____
_____
_____
_____
_____
_____
_____
_____

# 166

# 167

# 168

SUBJECT :

# 169

IDEAS :

SUBJECT :

IDEAS :

SUBJECT :

# 171

SUBJECT :

IDEAS :

_____
_____
_____
_____
_____
_____
_____
_____

_____
_____
_____

SUBJECT :

_____
_____
_____
_____
_____
_____
_____
_____
_____
_____

# 173

IDEAS :

SUBJECT :

174

SUBJECT :

175

IDEAS :

SUBJECT :

177

178

IDEAS :

SUBJECT :

179

# 180

_____
_____
_____
_____
_____
_____
_____
_____
_____
_____
_____
_____

SUBJECT :

_____
_____
_____
_____
_____
_____
_____
_____
_____
_____
_____

181

IDEAS :

SUBJECT :

# 182

IDEAS :

_____
_____
_____
_____
_____
_____
_____
_____
_____

_____
_____
_____

SUBJECT :

_____
_____
_____
_____
_____
_____
_____
_____
_____
_____
_____
_____

# 183

_____
_____
_____
_____
_____
_____
_____
_____

_____
_____
_____

SUBJECT :

_____
_____
_____
_____
_____
_____
_____
_____
_____
_____
_____
_____

## 184

IDEAS :

SUBJECT :

IDEAS :

SUBJECT :

186

187

188

189

IDEAS :

SUBJECT :

## 190

SUBJECT :

IDEAS :

SUBJECT :

192

IDEAS :

SUBJECT :

193

194

195

IDEAS :

SUBJECT :

# 197

IDEAS :

SUBJECT :

198

199

# 200

SUBJECT :

201

IDEAS :

IDEAS :

SUBJECT :

202

203

IDEAS :

SUBJECT :

IDEAS :

SUBJECT :

205

_____

_____

_____

_____

_____

_____

_____

_____

_____

_____

_____

_____

_____

_____

_____

_____

_____

_____

_____

_____

_____

_____

_____

_____

_____

_____

_____

IDEAS :

SUBJECT :

207

IDEAS :

SUBJECT :

209

# 210

211

IDEAS :

SUBJECT :

212

# 213

IDEAS :

_____
_____
_____
_____
_____
_____
_____
_____
_____

_____
_____
_____

SUBJECT :

_____
_____
_____
_____
_____
_____
_____
_____
_____
_____
_____
_____
_____
_____

# 214

# 215

IDEAS :

_____
_____
_____
_____
_____
_____
_____
_____
_____

_____
_____
_____

SUBJECT :

_____
_____
_____
_____
_____
_____
_____
_____
_____
_____
_____
_____
_____
_____

IDEAS :

SUBJECT :

IDEAS :

_____
_____
_____
_____
_____
_____
_____
_____
_____
_____
_____
_____
_____

SUBJECT :

_____
_____
_____
_____
_____
_____
_____
_____
_____
_____
_____
_____

218

IDEAS :

SUBJECT :

219

IDEAS :

SUBJECT :

# 221

IDEAS :

_____
_____
_____
_____
_____
_____
_____
_____
_____
_____

_____
_____
_____

SUBJECT :

_____
_____
_____
_____
_____
_____
_____
_____
_____
_____
_____
_____

# 222

IDEAS :

SUBJECT :

223

224

IDEAS :

SUBJECT :

# 225

SUBJECT :

# 226

IDEAS :

SUBJECT :

# 227

IDEAS :

_____
_____
_____
_____
_____
_____
_____
_____
_____

_____
_____
_____

SUBJECT :

_____
_____
_____
_____
_____
_____
_____
_____
_____
_____
_____
_____

IDEAS :

SUBJECT :

# 229

# 230

IDEAS :

SUBJECT :

231

IDEAS :

SUBJECT :

# 233

_____
_____
_____
_____
_____
_____
_____
_____

_____
_____
_____
_____

SUBJECT :

_____
_____
_____
_____
_____
_____
_____
_____
_____
_____
_____
_____

234

235

IDEAS :

SUBJECT :

237

# 238

IDEAS :

_____

_____

_____

_____

_____

_____

_____

_____

_____

_____

_____

SUBJECT :

239

IDEAS :

SUBJECT :

IDEAS :

SUBJECT :

IDEAS :

SUBJECT :

IDEAS :

_____
_____
_____
_____
_____
_____
_____
_____

_____
_____
_____

SUBJECT :

_____
_____
_____
_____
_____
_____
_____
_____
_____
_____
_____

243

SUBJECT :

# 244

IDEAS :

_____
_____
_____
_____
_____
_____
_____
_____

_____
_____
_____

SUBJECT :

_____
_____
_____
_____
_____
_____
_____
_____
_____
_____
_____
_____

IDEAS :

_____
_____
_____
_____
_____
_____
_____
_____
_____

_____
_____
_____

SUBJECT :

_____
_____
_____
_____
_____
_____
_____
_____
_____
_____
_____

IDEAS :

SUBJECT :

# 247

IDEAS :

SUBJECT :

248

IDEAS :

SUBJECT :

249

IDEAS :

SUBJECT :

# 251

_____
_____
_____
_____
_____
_____
_____
_____

_____
_____
_____

SUBJECT :

_____
_____
_____
_____
_____
_____
_____
_____
_____
_____
_____
_____

252

IDEAS :

_____
_____
_____
_____
_____
_____
_____
_____
_____
_____
_____
_____

SUBJECT :

# 253

IDEAS :

_____
_____
_____
_____
_____
_____
_____
_____
_____

_____
_____
_____

SUBJECT :

_____
_____
_____
_____
_____
_____
_____
_____
_____
_____
_____

254

# 255

256

IDEAS :

SUBJECT :

257

# 258

IDEAS :

SUBJECT :

259

IDEAS :

SUBJECT :

# 261

IDEAS :

_____
_____
_____
_____
_____
_____
_____
_____
_____
_____

_____
_____
_____
_____

SUBJECT :

_____
_____
_____
_____
_____
_____
_____
_____
_____
_____
_____

IDEAS :

SUBJECT :

# 263

SUBJECT :

IDEAS :

SUBJECT :

265

# 266

IDEAS :

_____
_____
_____
_____
_____
_____
_____
_____
_____
_____
_____

SUBJECT :

_____
_____
_____
_____
_____
_____
_____
_____
_____
_____
_____
_____

IDEAS :

SUBJECT :

# 268

IDEAS :

SUBJECT :

269

SUBJECT :

IDEAS :

_____
_____
_____
_____
_____
_____
_____
_____
_____
_____
_____
_____

SUBJECT :

_____
_____
_____
_____
_____
_____
_____
_____
_____
_____
_____
_____

271

IDEAS :

SUBJECT :

273

# 274

IDEAS :

SUBJECT :

275

IDEAS :

SUBJECT :

276

277

278

# 279

IDEAS :

SUBJECT :

# 280

IDEAS :

_____
_____
_____
_____
_____
_____
_____
_____

_____
_____
_____

SUBJECT :

_____
_____
_____
_____
_____
_____
_____
_____
_____
_____
_____

281

IDEAS :

_____
_____
_____
_____
_____
_____
_____
_____
_____

_____
_____
_____

SUBJECT :

_____
_____
_____
_____
_____
_____
_____
_____
_____
_____
_____
_____
_____

IDEAS :

_____
_____
_____
_____
_____
_____
_____
_____
_____

_____
_____
_____

SUBJECT :

_____
_____
_____
_____
_____
_____
_____
_____
_____
_____
_____
_____

283

284

IDEAS :

SUBJECT :

# 285

IDEAS :

SUBJECT :

# 286

IDEAS :

SUBJECT :

287

# 288

IDEAS :

_____
_____
_____
_____
_____
_____
_____
_____
_____

_____
_____
_____

SUBJECT :

IDEAS :

SUBJECT :

IDEAS :

SUBJECT :

IDEAS :

_____
_____
_____
_____
_____
_____
_____
_____
_____
_____
_____
_____

SUBJECT :

_____
_____
_____
_____
_____
_____
_____
_____
_____
_____
_____
_____

IDEAS :

SUBJECT :

293

294

295

_____
_____
_____
_____
_____
_____
_____
_____
_____
_____
_____

SUBJECT :

_____
_____
_____
_____
_____
_____
_____
_____
_____

296

SUBJECT :

297

298

# 299

IDEAS :

SUBJECT :

# 300

IDEAS :

IDEAS :

SUBJECT :

# 301

SUBJECT :

302

IDEAS :

SUBJECT :

# 303

# 304

305

# 306

# 307

# 308

# 309

_____
_____
_____
_____
_____
_____
_____
_____
_____

_____
_____
_____

SUBJECT :

_____
_____
_____
_____
_____
_____
_____
_____
_____
_____
_____

# 310

IDEAS :

_____

_____

_____

_____

_____

_____

_____

_____

_____

_____

_____

_____

SUBJECT :

_____

_____

_____

_____

_____

_____

_____

_____

_____

_____

_____

_____

_____

311

# 312

# 313

# 314

# 315

_____
_____
_____
_____
_____
_____
_____
_____
_____
_____
_____
_____

SUBJECT :

_____
_____
_____
_____
_____
_____
_____
_____
_____
_____

# 316

317

318

# 319

IDEAS :

SUBJECT :

320

IDEAS :

SUBJECT :

321

# 322

# 323

SUBJECT :

324

# 325

# 326

IDEAS :

SUBJECT :

327

SUBJECT :

# 328

SUBJECT :

329

# 330

# 331

332

IDEAS :

SUBJECT :

# 333

IDEAS :

_____
_____
_____
_____
_____
_____
_____
_____
_____
_____

_____
_____
_____

SUBJECT :

_____
_____
_____
_____
_____
_____
_____
_____
_____
_____
_____

334

# 335

# 336

IDEAS :

_____
_____
_____
_____
_____
_____
_____
_____

_____
_____
_____

SUBJECT :

_____
_____
_____
_____
_____
_____
_____
_____
_____
_____
_____

337

SUBJECT :

IDEAS :

SUBJECT :

IDEAS :

_____
_____
_____
_____
_____
_____
_____
_____
_____

_____
_____
_____

SUBJECT :

_____
_____
_____
_____
_____
_____
_____
_____
_____
_____
_____
_____

# 340

# 341

IDEAS :

SUBJECT :

342

# 343

# 344

IDEAS :

SUBJECT :

# 345

# 346

IDEAS :

SUBJECT :

# 347

_____
_____
_____
_____
_____
_____
_____
_____

_____
_____
_____

_____
_____
_____
_____
_____
_____
_____
_____
_____

348

# 349

IDEAS :

SUBJECT :

IDEAS :

_____
_____
_____
_____
_____
_____
_____
_____
_____
_____
_____

SUBJECT :

_____
_____
_____
_____
_____
_____
_____
_____
_____
_____
_____

# 351

# 352

IDEAS :

SUBJECT :

# 353

IDEAS :

SUBJECT :

354

# 355

_____
_____
_____
_____
_____
_____
_____
_____
_____
_____
_____

SUBJECT :

_____
_____
_____
_____
_____
_____
_____
_____
_____
_____
_____

# 356

IDEAS :

SUBJECT :

357

# 358

IDEAS :

SUBJECT :

# 359

# 360

IDEAS :

SUBJECT :

# 361

SUBJECT :

362

SUBJECT :

# 363

IDEAS :

_____
_____
_____
_____
_____
_____
_____
_____
_____
_____

_____
_____
_____

SUBJECT :

_____
_____
_____
_____
_____
_____
_____
_____
_____
_____
_____

# 364

IDEAS :

_____

_____

_____

_____

_____

_____

_____

_____

_____

_____

_____

SUBJECT :

_____

_____

_____

_____

_____

_____

_____

_____

_____

_____

_____

_____

# 365

IDEAS :

SUBJECT :

notes

*notes*

# notes

notes

This Is Me:
Selfie Time !

Sunrise

Outfit
of the
Day

Black & White
Challenge

Wild Flowers

Portrait of
a Friend

Texture

Geometric
Colors

Take a Photo
of One of
Your Hobbies

Jump !

A is for . . .

Remake of
a childhood
photo

Something Blue

Roses

A Pile
of
Things

Cat in Action !

Balloons

Candy

White
Background

Something
Broken

Remember Your Dreams ?

Something Moving Very Fast

Crystals

Insect in the Garden

Supermarket Shelves

Look What I Made

Lens Flare

Baby Animals

10 Day Challenge: Collect Nr. 0 to 9

Take a Photo of Your Favorite Plant

What's
That Bird
Doing?

Someplace
I've Never
Been Before

Seashells

Look
At My
Shoes

Saucy Juicy
Drizzling
Delicious Yummy

Live
Concert

Climb a Tree

Home
Made
Food

Reflections

The
Oldest Car
In Town

Pet a Dog !

Lay on the
Ground

The
City
I Live In

Path
Through
the Woods

Shiny Metal

My
Comfy Bed
Blanket & Pillows

A
Long
Exposure

Animal
in the
Clouds

Fallen Leaves

A
Lonely
Building

What
Are You
Collecting ?

My
Favorite
Cafe

Rainbows

Hearts

In
the
Dark

Graffiti:
Art on the
Streets

Making a
small thing
HUGE

The
Movement
of Water

Lunch time !

Confetti !

Candles

Visit
A
Farm

Children

It's
My
Birthday !

On the Road

What is
That Statue
About ?

It's
Christmas
Time

Look Up !

Abandoned
Building

A
Beautiful
Bicycle

Square
Photo

Shadows

Favorite
Record
Sleeve

Something
Goes
Wrong

That
Horse is Very
Close

Doughnuts

Through
the
Window

It's
Cold
Outside

Someone
You
Love

Blurry
Can Be
Better

| | |
|---|---|
| Fire ! | Alphabeth Photo A to Z 26 Day Challenge |
| Eyes Up Close | Who is Getting Married ? |
| Play time ! | The Herbs in the Garden |
| My Favorite Place in the World | White on White |
| Chickens | Write With Ribbon |

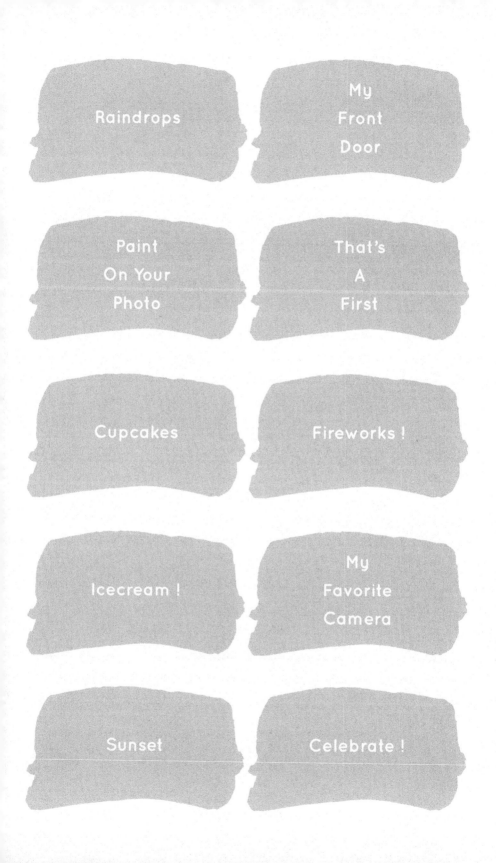

Made in the USA
Las Vegas, NV
08 December 2024

13661617R00213